Ava Dreams of Water

By Nancy Moss

Illustrated by Sara McCall Ephron

Special thanks to Derek O'Neill, Nancy Santullo, Michele Fitch, Sandra Squires, Charissa Barton, Lynn Anne Scalzi, and Jordan Ephron, for helping to make this book possible.

Nancy Moss lives in Los Angeles with her teenage twin sons and her occasionally bossy cat. She is a former film executive and screenwriter who strongly believes that everyone should follow their dreams!

Sara McCall Ephron writes, illustrates, and teaches art. She would love to live near a tropical ocean someday but in the meantime, is happy to enjoy long autumn walks with her family and dog Rosie, along the Hudson River in NYC. See more of Sara's illustration at **www.saramccallephron.com**

ISBN: 978-0-9969463-0-8

Design and Layout: Jordan Ephron
Additional Design and Layout: Charity Capili

Happy Platypus Press
avadreamsofwater@gmail.com
www.avadreamsofwater.com

For Betsy and love that flows forever...

Ava dreams of water. The water of the ocean.
The water in her fish tank. The water she and her
brother fill balloons with and throw at each other.

Water helps Ava start her day.

At school, a visitor named Jane comes to Ava's class. Jane asks, "What would it be like if you didn't have clean water to drink, or to take a bath, or to flush the toilet in your bathroom?"

Josh, the boy who sits next to Ava, giggles. Ava's friend Kate says, "Not fun!"

Jane tapes pictures on the wall of a village called Yomybato, deep in the rainforest of Peru. "Yomybato is a very beautiful place but people have to carry water a long distance, and it's not very healthy." She holds up a bottle filled with light brown liquid. "This is the water that children bring to school."

A few kids in the class shout, "yuck!" and "ick!"

"The people in Yomybato are building a bridge, made of rocks, pipes, and strong wire cables," Jane says. "Water will come from the other side of the river, then run through big tubs of stones and sand that clean it. That's called 'slow sand filtration.'"

"Very interesting!" says Kate.

"The villagers need a little more help to finish the bridge," Jane says. "So, how would you all like to pitch in?"

"That's crazy!" Josh says. "We don't know how to build a bridge!"

Jane smiles. "Well, kids can do a lot of amazing things." Jane points to one of the photos. "That's Juan. He takes people across the river in his family's boat, guiding it through the water with a long paddle. That's an important job, isn't it?"

Ava stares at the photo and thinks about what riding in Juan's boat would be like.

"There's an important job this class could have," Jane says. "Would you like to raise some money to help the people in Peru finish the bridge?"

All the kids think that sounds like a great idea.

"Let's see," Ms. Jones, Ava's teacher says. "Should we have a bake sale, or a car wash? Maybe we can put on a play and sell tickets? Let's vote!"

Everyone, including Ava, chooses the bake sale. "Ok, we'll have it this Friday," Ms. Jones says. "No eating the cake and cookies before you bring them to school!"

That night, Ava dreams of water, but this time the water is the river that Juan crosses in his boat. Ava is very surprised to see him! Juan looks up and grins. "Hello, Ava," he says.

"How do you know my name?" Ava asks.

"Because I met you today, in your class," Juan laughs. "Remember? Do you like my boat?"

"I do! Is it fun helping people get to the village?"

"Yes," says Juan, "except my little brother makes me take him along every time."

"That sounds like my brother," Ava says. "He just learned to ride a bike and now he keeps following me!"

Juan smiles. "I have to get someone across the river… Goodnight, Ava."

"Ok, bye." Ava watches Juan float away.

In the morning, Ava tells her parents how she saw Juan and talked to him. Her father says, "You've got a great imagination, honey!"

Ava's brother Sam laughs. Her mother tells him to stop. "That's wonderful, Ava," she says, but Ava feels like her whole family thinks it was just a dream.

At school, Ava thinks about Juan. The class decides what to bring for the bake sale that Friday. Ava raises her hand. "I'll make lemon boats… Oh, I mean lemon bars," says Ava, "not boats… I guess I was daydreaming."

That night, Ava hopes she can talk to Juan again. Closing her eyes, she wonders what Juan's life is like. Deep into her sleep, Ava sees Juan helping his mother gather something that looks like big green beans. He looks up and greets Ava.

"Welcome back! Are you hungry?"

"What are you picking?" Ava asks.

"It's called pacay," Juan says. "We open up the pods to get to the seeds inside. They're covered with a delicious white, fluffy pulp."

"We have a lemon tree in our backyard," Ava says.

"Ah!" Juan waves his arm and laughs. "This is my backyard!"

"I'm making lemon bars for the bake sale my class is having to raise money for your water bridge," Ava tells him.

"Thank you!" Juan says. "We're almost done but we could use some help. Hey, do you think I'd like those lemon bars?"

"They're a lot better than the ones you buy in a store. Do you have stores here?" Ava asks.

"No. All our food comes from the trees, and our gardens, and the animals we raise and hunt," Juan tells her. "Do you want me to show you around?"

"That would be great!" Ava says.

Just then, Juan's mother calls to him. "Juan, I need you to help your brother!"

"Well, I've got to go, Ava. Where's your brother?" Juan asks.

"He's sleeping. Like I am… I think," Ava says.

Juan laughs. "You talk pretty well for someone who's asleep."

"I hope I see you again, Juan," Ava says.

"Oh, you will," Juan calls out as he runs off.

During the week, Ava and her classmates get ready for the bake sale. Every night, after she falls asleep, Ava meets Juan in Yomybato. He shows her his house and his small one-room school, built of wood and other things from the forest.

Ava sees the toys that Juan and his friends play with. There are marbles, bows and arrows, and sticks and rocks they find around the village.

"We play some of the same games the older people in our families played when they were kids," Juan tells Ava. "Look! There are my friends, kicking a soccer ball!"

Ava says, "Hey, I play soccer! There's a lot that's different here in Yomybato, but some things that are almost the same as in my town!"

One night when Ava is visiting Juan, he takes her to the river where the villagers are building the water bridge. Wire holds the pipes in place. The bottom part of the bridge, which sits on each side of the riverbank, is made from rocks and strong cement.

"I wish it was the kind of bridge you can walk across," Juan says. "Maybe someday I'll build one of those!"

Juan tells Ava how the people carry the water a long distance to their homes. Soon they'll be able to drink from fountains, called "tap stands," at every house in the village.

"We're also going to have toilets that flush!" Juan says, very excited. Ava is glad for him. She's never seen anyone so happy about toilets!

"You're lucky you've always had them," Juan says. Ava thinks about how true that is.

"Very lucky," she says.

Ava tries to tell her family about what Juan has shown her. Her brother Sam says, "You're nutty, Ava!"

"She's just a dreamer," Ava's father says, "and there's nothing wrong with that." Ava decides that from now on she's going to keep her visits with Juan to herself.

The bake sale is a big success. Ava's teacher places empty water bottles around the table for people to put extra donations inside. It's a great way to explain to the customers all about how Juan's village needs clean water. Ava and her friends raise $200.00 to send to Peru!

Jane comes to the school and thanks all the kids. She tells them that the water bridge is almost finished and that their bake sale money will really help!

Over the next couple of weeks, while she sleeps, Juan shows Ava the progress on the bridge.

Juan and his friends help to carry rocks and other materials.
Soon the bridge is finished!

Jane visits school again and shows the kids pictures of water flowing in the village of Yomybato. Ava sees Juan and his friends drinking from the wonderful tap stands made of river stones and cement. She thinks about how happy Juan looks. She can't wait to talk to him that night.

At bedtime, Ava lays her head on her pillow, smiles, and closes her eyes.

Ava dreams of water. She sees the river that Juan brings his boat across, but he's not in it. Ava waits and waits for Juan to visit her again.

Suddenly, she wakes up. Ava sees that it's still dark outside her window. She tries to go back to sleep, hoping Juan will appear, but Ava just tosses and turns.

In the morning, Ava tells her mother she doesn't want breakfast because she feels dizzy, and asks if she can stay home from school.

"No fair!" Sam says. "Then I'm staying home too!"

"I'm afraid not, buddy," Ava's mom tells him. She puts her palm on Ava's forehead and asks if she's really sick.

"Well, I'm sad. I didn't see Juan last night."

"Oh, Ava. I'm sure you will again," her mother says.

"I'm worried something is wrong. I always see Juan there!" Ava says. "You don't understand!! Maybe someone will believe me at school!"

When Ava gets to her classroom, she looks around at her friends and teacher. "Forget it," she thinks to herself. "Maybe I am nutty!" Ava tries not to think about Juan but can't help wondering where he is. That night, Ava hopes she might see Juan while she sleeps, but Juan never shows up.

Juan dreams of water.

He sees a girl watering plants in a garden. There are trees and grass that are very different from Yomybato. The girl looks up. It's Ava.

"Juan! I'm so happy you're here!"

"I've come to see what your life is like, Ava. I'm sorry I haven't been around. All the kids in the village have been busy learning about the new water. Oh, and we love the toilets!" Juan and Ava both laugh.

"You know," says Juan, "our dreams are like the bridge that brought the water. They bring us to each other."

"For real, Juan?" Ava asks.

"Well, I'm here, right? Come on, show me around, Ava."

Ava smiles. "Let's go," she says.

YOMYBATO

Children in Yomybato.

Clean water flowing!

Helping to build the suspension bridge.

Bringing people across the river.

Boats carrying pipes for the suspension bridge.

A sink at school.

The classroom in Yomybato.

Online Search Topics

Here's a list of search topics for learning more about the Peruvian Amazon, the people who live there, and the quest for clean water around the world.

- Amazon Rainforest

- Peruvian Amazon

- Manu National Park

- Wildlife in Manu National Park

- Yomybato

- Matsigenka
  (the indigenous people of the Amazon basin jungle in southeast Peru)

- Clean Drinking Water

- Clean Water Projects

- Clean Water Technology

- Slow Sand Filtration

- World Water Day

- Earth Day

- Climate Change

- Biodiversity

- Rainforest Flow

How Can You Help?

There are so many causes that need your help. What project can you raise money for? It can be something far away or in your own town!

Bake Sale
Everyone loves home-baked goodies! Help out in the kitchen and bring your favorites to school to raise money for a good cause!

Healthy Snack Sale
Promote healthy eating and fundraise at the same time! Package nuts, seeds, and dried fruits and sell in packages. Offer fresh fruit, plain popcorn, and whole-wheat pretzels. What are your favorite healthy snacks?

Fun Run/Walk
Organize a run or walk around your schoolyard or playground. Have your family and their friends donate an amount of money for each lap you run or walk. What a great way to spread the word about exercise and health while you fundraise!

Yard Sale, or Used Book Sale, or Plant Sale
We all have things we no longer need that someone could use. Gather items that you can sell together with your friends and classmates. Ask your parents what they'd like to donate. A used book sale is a great way to share books you've liked with others, and pick up some new-to-you titles! Another idea is to have a "green" sale of plants, seeds, blubs, and flowers. Ask for donations from local nurseries and garden stores.

Put on a Play or Talent Show

A fun way to raise money is to put on a show and sell tickets. Your class can write something about the project you are trying to fund, or act out a favorite story. A talent show is a wonderful way to preform anything you like. Do you play an instrument or sing? Maybe you make funny voices! Everyone has a talent!

Coin Collection or Recycle Collection

Put out empty water bottles at your fundraisers for people to donate coins, or keep a big jar on your teacher's desk where everyone can drop spare change. You can also collect cans and bottles over a few weeks' time and have a parent or teacher take them to a recycling center.

Partner with Local Restaurant/Business

Find out if a restaurant or store in your neighborhood would like to help. They could put up signs about your fundraiser and hold a dinner (if a restaurant) or a day (if a store) when part of the money they make will be donated to your cause. Make flyers and spread the word!

More About Clean Water

Ava Dreams Of Water is inspired by the work of the non-profit organization Rainforest Flow, and the water system they have helped build in the Peruvian Amazon village of Yomybato with support from SQ Foundation.

"Water is the most basic element to life yet over 800,000 million people still live without access to clean water. The Matsigenka children living in the protected Manu Rainforest of Peru had no access to clean water. They were oftentimes sick from drinking unclean water and living with rustic sanitation conditions. Parents in Yomybato and other villages in Manu asked us to help create a better life and healthy future for their children. Manu is one of the most biologically diverse regions in the world. For this forest to survive, it will need an active healthy indigenous population.

Derek O'Neill and the SQ-Foundation have been instrumental in helping us bring clean water to these remote indigenous tribes since 2003. We are forever grateful for his vision and support."

— Nancy Santullo, Founder of Rainforest Flow

Learn more about Rainforest Flow at **www.rainforestflow.org** For more information on SQ Foundation, and the work they support around the world, visit **www.sq-foundation.org**.

CPSIA information can be obtained at www.ICGtesting.com
Printed in the USA
BVIW12n1548071217
501889BV00013B/133

RESOURCES